Triumph over Grief

COMPILED BY
CHERIE BARNES

Triumph Over Grief

Copyright © 2019 Cherie Barnes.

All rights reserved. Printed in the United States of America. No part of this book may be used or reproduced in any manner whatsoever without written permission except in the case of brief quotations em- bodied in critical articles or reviews.

Published by :

Relentless Publishing House, LlC

www.relentlesspublishing.com

ISBN: 978-1948829274

First Edition: July 2019

10 9 8 7 6 5 4 3 2 1

TABLE CONTENTS

Foreword — 1

Chapter 1: Light in the Storm — 5

Chapter 2: The Last One Standing — 13

Chapter 3: Turning Pain Into Purpose — 21

Chapter 4: Fathered But Daddyless — 30

Chapter 5: Still Standing — 39

About the Authors — 45

FOREWORD

We all experience losses in our lives. We are now at a tipping point in the world where we are bombarded with stories, images, and experiences of grief, loss, and trauma. Not knowing what to do, who to go to, no immediate resources to help us process and manage our emotions, we inevitably do nothing. We allow the pain to hold us hostage in our matrix-surrounded in another space or time before the pain.

Because we are not trained or educated to deal with our losses, our worldview is challenged. We are learning to accept existence in a death-denial society that forces us to suppress our feelings and continue living as if nothing happened. This of course is not possible. As a therapist, I can vehemently say, our human state won't allow it. It will do whatever is necessary to be acknowledged and heard. Our learning has to expand to recognize that grief can't just be buried along with the person. What we need instead are tools to assist us in finding ways to shift what has happened to us.

In my practice, I have worked with and seen clients in the throes of their grief. It is a privilege to witness and create a safe container for them. Heart wrenching at times, this granting of access by a client into their world is an honor. When clients show up and acknowledge that they need help, it is a strength. More than that, it is an indicator that they have not lost hope. This is where there magic happens.

I remember when this phenomenal energy filled with magic showed up. She was invited to one of my women empowerment business gatherings by a colleague. I noticed her quiet reserve during the gathering, attentively taking notes, and you knew something brewing.

Great, I thought, she is connecting and getting something from the meetup. As a therapist and business coach, when I host events, I ask everyone to bring their knowledge and expertise to the events so that they can be utilized in a cooperative way- everyone benefits from the presence and knowledge of everyone. At the end of the event, this person came up to me and said, "I need to work with you."

That person was author, speaker, therapist, and grief advocate, Cherie Barnes. When Cherie begin to share her beautiful story of love, loss, and trauma with me, I knew that I would assist her with whatever she needed to begin her transformation and ultimate journey to recover from her devastating loss of losing a loved one.

Cherie initially had a goal to curate a book to assist her daughter, Nia, who is now a published author, in healing from her loss of a father figure. Cherie expressed her frustration, because there were limited to no resources available for her specific need. What I heard in her goal was also a space for her own healing and the healing of others. We talked about turning her story into a book. Hesitant, yet determined, Cherie began her self work of healing for herself and others. She decided if it wasn't available, then she would create it. Thus, her first book, 12 Lessons of HealingThrough Grief, a guide for healing and hope from grief was born. Soon to follow was her sequel, Conversations With God, a devotional on dealing with loss. The third book to this trilogy, a co-authored project & Amazon #1 Best Seller, both in the U.S. and U.K, The Awake Anthology, a book of empowerment for women showcases Cherie's ability to share her personal experiences in a way that aids others in renewal and growth. Now in this fourth book, Triumph Over Grief, an assortment of stories that showcase challenges from grief to triumph, Cherie acts as a transformative agent by challenging us to allow grief to be a process of transformation, rather than a location of holding.

In life, we all have choices. When we are faced with difficulties and losses, we can choose to let go, to stay still, or move towards greater, within our pain. It is totally up to you. What can help in your transition is acceptance of the situation that you are confronting. While it may not be easy, this book can act as your roadmap to help you face it with inner strength and hope-where you can begin to embrace life and find joy again.

You may have had one of those moments when the world seems to have stopped and all you feel is numb. I've felt it and so has Cherie. While we may want the world to stop moving, it won't, so we owe it to ourselves to learn how to move with it. Cherie was able to do this by turning her loss into growth and helping others do the same. That is the purpose behind this book.

I am honored that Cherie asked me to write the foreword to this latest work of guidance in the grief process. I see her use of self during this process as a vehicle. One that allows us to do our work by committing to our wellbeing first and taking one step at a time. Cherie has taken us behind the red curtain, given us full disclosure, and vulnerability while processing her own loss from learning how to live, embrace happiness, and ultimately love again. Use this book as your tool and share the process with others. I wish you hope, health, and healing on your journey from grief to triumph.

Dr. Sonia Kennedy
The Biz Therapist
Author, Therapist & Life Coach
Empowering Wellness 360

CHAPTER ONE

Light in the Storm

A storm has been defined as: disturbance of the normal condition of the atmosphere, manifesting itself by winds of unusual force or direction. (**www.dictionary.com**)

This is something you see on the news during the weather report. It ruins your outdoor activities, causing you to make a revision to an already set agenda. Until just recently, I'd never compare the weather, to a chapter in my life.

I'll speak for myself when I claim you grow with expectations of "what life will be like". You imagine "joys" of accomplishments quite frankly. YES, I wore the rose-colored glasses. It didn't matter what occurred around me, I envisioned the brighter side of the road. Of course, I knew, "things happened" and as you age, you hear the "stories" from those around that have the experienced life. You soon realize there is disappointment, loss and the darkness a person will inevitable encounter, but it is not until "Life Happens" do you truly understand.

While revisiting the years in my head, I've recognized this

self-defining moment, the one that clearly spoke to God doing a remarkable miracle in my life. I'm able to formulate a true smile and profess, "I'm a woman who by the grace of GOD was able to rise out of a black hole."

This particular part of the journey entailed a dim path that I describe as painful both spiritually and emotionally. It was as though both my mind and body was aggressively hijacked -- unwillingly. One may inquire, "How does that happen? When did that type of storm originate?" At that juncture, I too was baffled by those very questions. The Michelle that was no longer existed. You may ask, "What is the back story?"

It began almost four years ago:
August 20, 2015, a day forever etched in my mind. Rewind: almost lunchtime, at the office preparing for a lunch outing, I suddenly experienced several hot flashes, my face literally burning, it was as if there was a malfunction with my body. Fortunate for me, I was blessed to be in the presence of nurses (I will forever call those two my gifts on earth). One quickly assessed me and determined action steps needed to be taken. After recruiting another nurse, I was quickly transported by taxi to the hospital. Little did I know, that very visit would turn into an admission.

Following the dreaded, 6-7 hours in the ER, literally dozens of tests, I received a preliminary diagnosis: "Based on all your tests, we have come to a provision diagnosis of MS—Multiple Sclerosis." While a team of doctors and residents swarmed around me like a case study in class, I disappeared into a state of shock. WHAT!!!??? I thought in my mind, "What does that mean?

The tears welled, but I mustered up the strength not to ball at that moment. In fact, I yelled inside to myself, "I refuse to be the spectacle, to an audience, no thank you to any sympathy." I now craved alone time to process, I'd fallen, like Alice in Wonderland down the hole, however mine was bottomless. Life became a world wind. I'd been admitted to a hospital from the ER. Hospital admission #1.

    I reverted to an infant state. I could no longer independently care for myself AT ALL. This literally happened within a 24-hour period. It's as though my body shut down. How many days passed from my real life? I recall laughter, walking, driving, cooking, clear vision and even the ability to shower. I remembered. Then the million dollar questions began to creep in my mind, "Why me? What did I do so wrong?" Entangled with the emotions of anger, despair, and sadness, I longed to know, "Who am I now? What do I do next?" My identity as a mother, wife, and woman was literally snatched from me within a moment. My mind was in turmoil, like a DVR replay. I keep telling myself "You are now labeled a disabled person." They provided us with literature to read on MS. I pushed it aside. I don't want to read that. I felt defeated. The statistics, unknown factors caused a huge knot in the pit of my stomach. This is actually the point I began to grieve me. Initially, denial crept within, numbness, fear, avoidance I knew all too well.

    Now looking back, when I thought about sickness, it was the over the counter, doctor's prescription that could provide me with that 7 to 10 day relief. This right here was something I knew nothing about. I mean you of course hear about diseases that infiltrate one's body. There's never a full understanding until it's you. Multiple Sclerosis was something that I saw when you filled out health conditions in the question, "Have you ever been diagnosed with the following....?"

While I've never been a person that claimed to be invincible, I would've never imagined this as a chapter in my book. For days, I intentionally retired from existing and allowed my grief to increase. Looking around, I was institutionalized in a place with schedules to welcome visitors, eat, shower and receive therapy, I became more depressed as the days passed. In darkness is where I temporarily resided. What felt like forever was actually less than a week.

Six days later, I was released home, prescription medications and a referral for OT/PT. Unfortunately, 6 days later, I experienced side effects to the medications, increase of internal symptoms as a result the ambulance was called, Hospital admission #2.

Within days, everything about me began changing. The roller coaster continued. My facial features actually shifted. The doctors called this Bell's Palsy. This is a condition in which the muscles on one side of your face become weak or paralyzed. Therefore, in additional to being given a diagnosis of an incurable disease, I now had a deformity of the face. Also, my vision was compromised and failing in one eye. I had limited mobility and unable to fully utilize my vocal skills. Really?!!!!...Here we go again, the rumbling of a coming storm.

A thunderstorm occurred when the doctor indicated, "We are recommending admission to a rehabilitation facility, you're not able to care for yourself."

Words circled in my head, CONFINMENT and PRISONER. I didn't know long I loomed in this mental space. Around me the world continued, and then in an instance I immediately froze like an ice sculpture. "WHO AM I, WHO AM I, AND WHO AM I? WAS I NOT A WIFE, MOTHER AND FULL-TIME WORKER DAYS AGO?!!!!!!!!!!! I no longer know. I don't care what the hospital admission paperwork indicated. Michelle McKinnie was not the same person that was initially admitted August 20th. A puddle of tears followed after I signed the paperwork (with assistance) to be snatched from my family.

Rehab admission: This experience was initially depressing. I refused to utilize the lights in my room, and remained in hibernation until my therapy appointments. I had to endure hours of occupational and physical therapy three times a day. I recall prior to the start of therapy one of the staffs warning me, "If you want to leave rehab you have to work." Rehabilitation life consisted of the following, learning to eat, fully speak, utilize my hands and walkng. I required both a wheel chair and walker to travel. It's a fight that requires determination and patience. Each day I thought I was doing better. My rehab doctor would respond, "You're doing much better, but you can't go yet." One step forward, two steps back. Frown!! "I'm ready to go!" echoed in my head. I hate this!!!!
The walls began to suffocate me and the annoyance of the staff continuing to encourage my participation in the life around me made me want to scream. My ongoing response "no" with a polite half-smile and honestly I wanted to say, "Leave me alone! Do you

see how I look? My face is deformed, I have a patch on my eye in a wheelchair, can hardly speak and I'm forced to eat puree food!!" My manners prevented me from speaking verbally acknowledging my true thoughts. What do you do when this is now your life? You secretly cry after the visitors leave and you turn all the lights off in the room. Personally, losing myself took an emotional toll on me and my life in all areas around. I realized that I became a person that withdrew during this in extremely stressful moment. I flip-flopped from wanting to receive assistance to preferring to sit on Victim Island of "Why Me?"

I can't recall exactly when it happened, but one day I knew I had to turn the pain into determination. I couldn't expect change if I never made any effort. Everyone around could pray all day BUT I had to do my part.

This is a part of my story when the light appeared in the storm. Marriage vows in action…."in sickness and in health." I'm forever grateful for my husband's heart during these trying times. I recalled the fear when the medical staff recommended admission to rehab. The anxiety grew as my eyes met his. I shook my head as if to say, "NOOOOOO!" My weakness was obvious. He grabbed my hand symbolizing protection. In addition to the medical staff, he was truly instrumental in nursing me to health. He pushed me when I attempted to pause. I can recall the waterfalls when I was unable to clean my own body. Gently wiping my tears, his musical words of encouragement provided the cultivation. He possessed the strength God gives married couples He blesses. My own pride had to take a back seat and my self-pity had to be extinguished like a fire preparing to grow.

While it took time, I slowly made movement to reclaim my life, I began to pray, read and meditate on things that allowed my worth to grow inside. Work. I began to live again. I turned on the light that had been shut off. I was no longer embarrassed to look at myself in the mirror. While I had a crooked smile, I said to myself, "You will get better." Those that loved and cared for me continued to fill my bucket when it was empty. My little daughter's voice, "When are you coming home?" provided a motivation from a daughter to mother. Yes, I had fallen and, in my mind, fallen hard, but I was reminded through this experience there is nothing God cannot restore. As I grew closer to Him, He clearly showed me a better way.

While this is not the end of my story, this is a peek into my life to show no matter what a situation may look like, nothing is permanent but our own thoughts should we let them take over. I pray this is an inspiration to show God's capability. I am now independent and can navigate on my own, I can't profess to declare I have my "old" life back. I say I've gained a new perspective on my life and purpose. I now feel an obligation to share with the world our limitless possibilities if we believe. However, believe includes work. While I'm still on the unpredictable journey in this life, I plant myself sit in a place of gratefulness focusing on the wellness of my mind body and spirit. It is a trio, which I must focus on daily:

1. Mind: What am I focused on? What do I think? What is causing mental stress am I willing to release it?
2. Body: What do I consume: healthy meals, hydrating my

body, and taking my vitamins? Am I physically active? Do I get proper rest?

3   Spirit: Am I spiritually full? What am I reading? What am I believing?

Together this regimen, if deliberately followed will play a role in my overall success. This will allow God to see my commitment to my life on earth.

Yes, I acknowledge what has been documented about my physical health, however, I don't let it control my life. I've continued day by day to relinquish what creates DIS-EASE. While it is not automatic, my actions are intentional. When I mess up (because there are those days), I get up anf shake it off and try again. I've learned to be generous to myself and accept "Good Enough". I'm not perfect and that's okay in my book.

This humble attitude, coupled with prayer and grace has allowed my health to be restored. I focus forward daily and look back as a reference. Not only has my faith increased, so has my desire to broadcast God's miracle in my life. This experience not only shaped me but showed me how He strategically collected my broken pieces for His good. What is next? It is a day by day walk.

-Michelle McKinnie

CHAPTER TWO

The Last One Standing

Death is universal, having no respect of a person's affluence or lack of, wealth or sovereignty, creed, culture, politricks or persona. I believe we can be and oftentimes are slaves to our grief and pain as it relates to loss and death. On September 14, 2017, I lost my mother and 33 days later on October 17, 2017, I would lose my final grandparent. It's been a tedious journey for me since I lost "Soldier", a title I affectionately gave my mom. Bertha M. Kemp had so many battles to fight in her lifetime and health was one of her most formidable challengers. It was an opponent that she'd reckoned with continuously and doggedly during various seasons of her life. She was optimistic, nontraditional, hard headed, stubborn and realistic about the pain and overall wrecking her body endured. Sometimes she would say in jest," I'm old and decrepit now. Time is dragging me down!" She knew this declaration would always get me to guffaw in deep laughter. We knew that despite her acknowledgement of life's blows, Soldier with a sly wink was cleverly clapping back with her mouth and her indomitable spirit. Get out of here; she wasn't just going to go gently into that good night. She gave every adversity a fierce challenge.

She'd study her illnesses, look in that dad- blasted medical book of hers reviewing the side effects of the medicine prescribed by the doctor and sometimes to her detriment, refused to take it. She knew best, and was determined to live and die on her own terms and had no qualms with suffering the consequences of her actions. She would go against the grain and decide the quality and methodology of how her life should be lived. Why not? She'd fought poverty, family dysfunction… losing her beloved dad when she was age 13 to alcoholism, fought to be educated and then to educate others. She was a bulwark, a great servant leader, top educator, community activist, social reformer, woman of great faith, mother, wife and friend.

Though her disposition was down home, she was also imbued with a regal air of boujee sophistication that drew lines in the sand. Of course, she wasn't letting Death become familiar with her. My momma wasn't common. Familiarity breeds contempt. She'd had her bouts, bruises, bumps…battles and counterattacked with even blows to racism, sexism, colorism, and lastly ageism. She was more than willing to fight back and stave off death. With these constant interruptions called life, my mom by sheer uncompromising will, the grace of God, her temerity and unwavering mindset was empowered to ignore the bell tolling and every sounding alarm! She kept herself here on planet earth longer than what some others would choose to endure or thought she could survive. She decreed, declared, rebuked, and called death to order as she spoke time back into her very life.

It would be a battle in response to every life's circumstance she'd endured and overcame prior to these uncircumcised Philistines called COPD, cervical cancer, congestive heart failure, rheumatoid arthritis, osteoarthritis, hiatal hernia, etc. Her method of bringing her five smooth stones and one slingshot to the fight made her a "bad shut yo mouth". She would do this thing her way. This disciplined mind and her organic responses to life is why she could and would overcome. Her fervent prayers and fortitude of strength enabled her arthritic knees to take her places that had no cartilage could carry her. She was an anomaly!

Her deep abiding love for her family, friends and community meant she wasn't ready to give up the ghost yet. So, by her sheer desire to live, her declarations and decrees over herself, she would continue to beat the odds with valor and on her on terms until she wouldn't. Dr. Seuss wrote about that. He spoke on the flying, the soaring, the passing, the winning and the glory! Oh, the places we will go, except when you don't! In hospital room C925 with only one eye opened because her recent stroke had closed the left eye permanently, without a mumbling word to say, she listened to me her daughter one last time. I affirmed her, called her blessed, and gave her permission to leave. She looked fixedly at me and her two granddaughters "Grammy's babies" as she called them. Though listening to me, I knew instinctively she was multitasking. She was hearing the diesels humming. It was time to board the train home to Jordan. Faith was her key. I knew she was ready to leave her fleshly baggage and cross over to the incorruptible. She was thanking the Lord... In my bones, I knew she was ready... it was oh the place she would go! Soldier was ready to "Go In". She took her own counsel on this one. Mom would often say, "Sometimes people just need you to just listen to them. They are not coming to you for advice. They just need you to listen" and so she listened.

The line on the beeping machine fell straight. Panic set in. My daughters look nervous. "What does that mean?" I kept asking! They had no answers for me. I was confused. It did not play out like scenes in the movies. No loud and continuous beep to signal the finality of one's existence. There was no regal pronouncement of what my taut and skittish muscles knew to be the truth. The nurse returned to the room

to gently say. "I'm so sorry honey, your mother is gone!
The word Gone seared into my consciousness like a red-hot poker... It repeated itself quickly, disrespectfully, intrusively..., Gone, Gone, GONE...

The very thing I feared was upon me, being a motherless child. I opened my mouth, spread my arms outward, fell backwards and wailed to the high heavens. The nurse and my daughters caught me. Oh, sweet Jesus, how can it be done JUST LIKE THAT... what do I do now? I have no mother, I'm motherless! And then the guttural growling came. I could hear the scream busting up my guts, roar across my teeth, gush out my mouth, rage through my soul, "Moooommmmmaaaa, Mooooooommmmmmmaaaaa!!!"

I'd heard this somewhere before. The same way, the very same tone, the exact texture. The frequencies of death had personally honed into my world. It was the same howl, I heard my matriarchal grandmother wail to the high heavens in 2000, when she laid her eyes upon her mother at the wake. It was haunting to hear our voices merge into one! How could my beloved grandmother chorus with me as her daughter crossed time to eternity to be with her? I'm convinced Grandma was acknowledging my grief while simultaneously welcoming her daughter home. They say the hearing is the last thing to go after a person is pronounced dead. I wondered if my pain put mom in conflict. Did she say one last earthly prayer for me in route to see her King and Lord? I sure would like to think so!

My friend Felecia Pearson Smith, a theologian and First Lady, assessed my experience like this, "Ummm, Girl that was the Ancestors!!" There is a picture that I've kept on my piano for years. It is a four generational photo taken when I was about 14 years old. It reflects the beauty of my maternal side of the family. We're all gazing at the camera; Great-grandma, Grandma, Mom and me. I suspect my dad took the picture. I am grateful for this treasured, very casual and nondescript moment in time. The gag is that all of us are only girls and each of us was close to our mothers. I personally witnessed the anguish of my grandmother and my mother at the loss of each of their moms. My grandmother Pecola original response was that she did not want to be here long after the death of her mother, Emma. She finally tapped into her support system of her brothers and sister in law to keep meaning in her life. But she died within seven years of her mother's death. Yup, seven is the number of completion and in the seventh year of her mother's death, grandma Pecola died suddenly as a result of a stroke. Upon my grandmother's death, my mom went into a deep depression, becoming a shell of her gregarious character and took to isolation. I suggested grief counseling. She concurred, acquiesced, committing herself to this process for a number of years. From time to time, when she needed maintenance counseling, she'd seek it.

And from time to time, I'd look at this framed picture sitting imposingly on my piano and think….Uggghhh, one day I will be the last one in this photograph. This day has come and now what?!! They say Death comes in threes and it did happen that way in the wake and dawn of mom's transition with Aunt Cee dying two weeks prior.

How I've cringed at and bemoaned every lost! My great-grandmother Emma World Speights departed life October 2000, my maternal grandmother, Feb 26, 2010, and now (Soldier) September 14, 2017.

We must soldier on, so after a huge family breakfast to honor my mom, we went to visit my paternal grandmother at the nursing home. The old girl was sharp even in her dementia! "Where yall coming from? Where yall been?" "Oh, we just went out to eat, just a family get together" replied my Aunt Juanita. "MMMHHHmmm," she replied, rolling her eyes with suspicion but she let the answer fly. Grandma wasn't no fool, never had been. Even in her dementia, her clap backs were classic and funny as all get out! Seeing her decline oftentimes made me sad. But today, I didn't dwell on that; I was intentional about my thoughts. I mused, Momma is gone but I'm so grateful, I still have grandma, my final grandparent. I lived in the precious moment, constantly taking pics. Little did I know that the death angel was trotting towards her! We had to endure hospice. Waiting on Death is not easy. It takes a toll on your mind and body. But out of it comes some of the most amazing moments, revelation of God's presence and power. You learn of your weaknesses, His strength, and your ability to survive, and thrive under pressure. It is the silver cord, the thread between life and death that you are privileged to bear. It doesn't necessarily feel like a privilege at the time.

In this process, I got a chance to sing songs to my grandmother and soothe her when she was really frightened, copartner with my family in one of the most intimate things of life that you can witness and participate in next to giving birth. In my mind they are close to the same thing. The Bible says mourn when new life arrives; rejoice when they go back to God.

We perceive that we won't come out of this thing alive. Thus, we put on layers and layers of grief and carry it around like itchy, sour sackcloths drenched in our own stench and sorrow. Sack cloths irritate our flesh, our spirits. Its purpose is for submission and dominance. Sometimes if we'd dare admit it, we are humiliated and tuckered out under Death's weight. We don't know how we'll last another day. We sit in ashes, pouring them on our heads; sometimes consuming and ruining our lives under the loss. Our grief is a burden born of our pain! We have no idea of how to turn mourning into joy. Our rhetoric, cries, and tears, makes it a struggle to pick up our bed and walk. We justify poor choices. We settle for hobbling with a limp or seeking the aid of a crutch. We're moving, but what are we moving to and where are we coming from? Movement does not equate growing. Even Jesus wrestled with the concept of His finiteness in the Garden of Gethsemane and the very thought of a violent separation of flesh and soul made Him sweat blood and cry tears. Yes, even the Good Shepherd needed to be ministered to by the angels for the preparation of, coexistence with and triumph over death. He needed to pray and have His inner circle watch and pray while He was in such a vulnerable state of choosing life or death. His friends went to sleep during one of the most pivotal points in His life. They inadvertently disappointed and hurt Him in their humanness.

According to Hebrew 9:27, we all have an appointment with death. The very thought of having an expiration date; our love ones having a shelf life, and the expectancy or unexpected surprise of death's intrusion can be daunting! Deaths tactics can be as bold as a raging bull in the china shop or wicked as stealing the breath of an infant. Whatsoever the method, the results can be maddening and deadly to the recipient and the survivor. It's duality to usher us into the presence of God can make us spiritually schizophrenic if we're honest. Death does sting, especially when our inability to stave it off allows it to rush into already empty places. Be honest, outside of purchasing life insurance, we don't consciously schedule the Grim Reaper into our already precarious or perfect lives.

Though the person we love may welcome death, make peace with it and see it as a loving friend, what of we who remain. This unwanted truce and alliance make us uncomfortable. I am no exception. I loosely use the word lose and lost. Is our love one really lost? Where did they go and why? Do we really know based on our faith? What of those who doubt? How do we come through this and not become lost ourselves? Here's my take away in a journey I am still navigating through. Be honest about your feelings with yourself and to others. Connect well to grieve well. Don't kick it with the scornful or seek the counsel of fools. Study the science of grieving ...why not, we study other subjects. Forgive yourself and others. Death can bring out the best and worst in us, unearthing buried dysfunctions. Pursue help by seeking out your Garden of Gethsemane crew. Don't "treat them" or toss them should they appear to fall asleep in your situation. They more than likely have your back and are definitely your gatekeepers. If you need clinical help, pursue that too. There is no shame in seeking professional counsel. Learn how to prepare for death by living well daily. Be proactive for others will die serving more grief to eat and consume. Loving people well and communicating effectively helps ease life's future woes because there will not be the sting of regret, disappointment of unfinished or ugly business when death reenters our lives.

      Listen, I stand on this side of glory knowing that Mom, Grandma and Great-grandma await me on distant shores. At my appointed time, I will reunite with them and not before. And with this shift in perspective I will strive to live my best life, avoid cigarettes to combat my grief and drop these 20 plus pounds, a crutch gleaned in the wake of a pain so deep that I allowed it to so easily beset me and literally weigh me down. Death stings but it will not kill me! For I choose not go gently into that good night!

-Valrie Kemp-Davis

CHAPTER THREE

Turning Pain Into Purpose

    The day my mother died; my life was forever changed. I didn't realize how deeply a person could hurt. My heart was broken. It was as if I could literally feel my heart being savagely ripped from my chest. Until then, I'd never truly been heartbroken. Although I knew enough about grief and loss that I expected to be sad and possibly depressed for a while, what I hadn't known was the physical toll grief would take on my body. Before my Mom's death, save for an auto-immune disease which was controlled with medication, my health was pretty good.

    On Tuesday November 8, 2011, at 5:04 am, I received a call: "Janis, this is your Father. Donna left us..." Words spoken to me by my Father, informing me that my Mother, Donna Jean Taylor, was no longer a living, breathing being. The woman who carried me in her womb for nearly 10 months, the person who took care of me my entire life, the woman who loved me at my most unlovable...DIED? What!? This was my reality. As sad and devastatingly painful as it was, it was real. My mother had fought a short battle with Colon Cancer. Christmas Eve, 2007 she felt a nagging pain in her shoulder that was so uncomfortable that she'd end up in the Urgent Care. That day changed the rest of our lives: she was diagnosed with Stage 4 Colon Cancer. Stage 4. After consulting with a couple of oncologists, she was told that the cancer was terminal, and she had about 6 months to live.

When a person is diagnosed at Stage 4 cancer, it means that the disease has spread to other organs. The colon cancer had spread to her liver. We knew what that meant; certain death. My mother began chemotherapy treatments in the spring in 2008. Through the grace of God, she remained employed during most of her battle with the disease. She was such a trooper! She'd go to chemo in the morning and report to work the same afternoon. I remember asking God to completely remove the cancer from her body, to reverse the diagnosis, and allow the chemo to completely kill all the cancer. What I learned, is that even though those prayers were not answered (at least, not in the way I'd hoped) God was still blessing her and us as a family.

God has an interesting way of showing up in the deepest of dark times. As much as I wanted to curse God during the most unimaginably horrible times in my life, I just couldn't. God constantly reminded me that no matter what I saw in front of me; all was well. God reminded me that my dear mother was His child first and that He was going to take care of her. I remember praying and asking God to take away all the cancer so that her scans would come back clear. Time and time again, that prayer went unanswered. Time...and time again. Finally, one day, my prayer changed. I no longer asked God to take away the cancer, though it was still my desire; instead, I prayed that God would give me the courage to accept His will for her life. HIS will; not mine. After praying that prayer, a sense of peace came over me. A peace that I truly cannot explain, nor did I understand at the time. Soon, I would realize that the peace I felt would be my saving grace during my mother's illness and for years to come. Little did I know, life was about to deliver a series of blows that would literally take my breath away, nearly end my life. Life has an interesting way of showing you how strong you are.

When the doctor told us that she was recommending hospice for my Mom, my health tanked. I was in the urgent care a week later for a "high-blood pressure episode", as the ER doctor called it. I was a person who traditionally had low blood pressure, not low enough to be concerned, but my normal readings never went above 90/60. That day in the urgent care, my reading was 183/151. At that point, my life would forever change. My faith, although faint, never wavered; not ever. I had quite a few questions for God, but I never doubted him. I knew that somehow, some way, I would survive. As my dear Mother's body grew weak and she could no longer fight, there was a huge hole forming in my heart; a hole in the shape of my Mother. How in the world was I supposed to live, the rest of my LIFE, without my Mother? Well, what I didn't know, I soon found out.

Knowing that one of the only people on this planet who has ever loved you, unconditionally, is dying, is understandably, earth-shattering. I literally felt the earth move underneath my feet. I didn't think about God and how awesome and powerful He is. I didn't think about how I needed to believe God's report instead of the doctors. The only thing I thought about was: MY MOTHER CANNOT DIE! I'm sure that reaction was a common one; what I wasn't sure about was how I was going to live on this earth without her. So much pain; what was the purpose?

Fast forward to the spring of 2012, our family was trying to move forward without our girl, but life was hard. I remember being numb and anxious all at once. I was in and out of the urgent care because of debilitating panic attacks. There were days that I could not function at work because, when the realization of my mother no longer being here hit me, I literally lost my breath. My father was so supportive of me during this time. He just sat and held me and allowed me to feel what I felt and cry when I needed to. He too was dealing with a huge loss; he and my mom had been together since they were kids. To add to the pain of grief, I'd previously left my marriage, a year after my mom was diagnosed. After going through years of child support court proceedings, which drained me emotionally and financially, the divorce was made final in the spring of 2012. Nearly a year after my mother's death; the death of my marriage was finalized. The lesson I learned during this painful process is that the end of a marriage, no matter how necessary it is, is the death of a relationship, dreams, and plans. Life, again, has an interesting way of showing you just how strong you are.

I don't recall much of 2012, as I was in a state of disbelief, numbness and panic the entire time. 2013 was somewhat uneventful. The panic and anxiety became a little more manageable and I'd begun to speak to and hear from God again. Throughout the previous couple of years since my mom's passing, I honestly don't remember hearing from Him very often, although, I know that He was with me the entire time. I remember asking God to show me how to turn the pain into purpose for my life. It was literally killing me, and I knew I had to live for my daughter, my family, my friends, but most of all, for myself.

The year 2014 began as an uneventful one …until. I was at work eating lunch with two of my friends. Scrolling through my dad's social media page that he'd created as a support group for widows/widowers and people who'd experienced loss. I read something that completely stopped me in my tracks. I remember dropping the sandwich I'd been eating and screaming "What!?" My father had posted to the group that "…today, we lost the matriarch of the family; Donna's mother died." Wait; what? Immediately, I called my dad, in hysterics, asking for what I'd just read to please not be true! Sadly, it was. 2 years and few months after my mom died; my dear grandmother passed away in her sleep. My grandmother, for a woman of 88 years, was in pretty good health. She lived alone and was pretty much independent. Her death was easier for me to accept, in a way, mainly because I was told that she "slept away" peacefully, which was her wish. However, it saddened me that she was in so much pain about losing my mom. Many of us in the family believe that she died of a broken heart, as she could never really come to grips with the loss of her first child, my mother. It's been said that no matter how old you become, you're still your parent's baby. My mother, though 61 years old when she died, was still my grandmother's baby. Still.

I was so numb; so much pain. What was the purpose? This was my conversation with God; "Why so much pain? What is the purpose? What are you saying to me, God? What??' The anxiety resurfaced with a vengeance. There were days when I thought I would die; literally leave this earth. There were times when I'd kiss my daughter goodnight as if it were the last time I'd ever see her. At that time, I could probably count the number of days I felt good, on one hand. I was a living, breathing (barely), mess; and no one knew it. I bargained, begged and pleaded with God for a healing from all the pain. I could not understand why I could not "get past" all the hurt. Again, I expected there to be sadness and grief, but not to the point of being stifled. And I was, literally, stifled. Everything had stopped. I lost interest in most things that previously brought me great joy, except for spending time with my daughter. For me, I thought, there was no purpose in enjoying life if it would not include my mother. My dad was amazing during this time. He was dealing with his own debilitating grief, he always found time to listen to me, comfort me and show love to me and my daughter. My dad was my person and he was always there. Always.

Besides God, my dad was my go-to guy. He was not a perfect father, and he knew it. He was real, raw and honest. Sometimes, brutally honest. During the years after my mom passed, I saw my dad change. He, like the rest of us, was sad. Most of the time, just sad. We had the most amazing "weepy" sessions, as he called them, whenever one or both of us was stifled by grief. He wasn't a religious man, at all, rather; he was spiritual. He would remind me that the "Higher Power" was there for us whenever we needed Him. My dad reminded me that God had a calling on my life that even the debilitating grief could not take away. Needless to say; my dad was my dude. In March of 2015, my dad called me over to his house, which was directly across the street from mine, and asked me to look at something. He'd been trying to write down a set of numbers, but whenever he put pen to paper, the numbers were inverted. Strange. He said he'd been feeling a little weird lately, which he said was probably due to some food he'd eaten a few days prior. About a week later, he told me he felt better and went back to his normal routine.

     On the morning of May 12, 2015, the day after Mother's Day, my dad rang my doorbell around 6:00am. What I saw when I opened the door completely shook me! My dad's face was drooping on one side and his speech was slurred. "Father!" I exclaimed while immediately grabbing him and pulling him inside the house. I knew what was happening; my father was having a stroke, right there at my front door. He tried to talk and tell me what was going on. I told him to be calm and that I'd get him to the hospital. I went into action, called my brother and aunt and explained to them what happened, as I needed someone to sit with my daughter and get her ready for school. I can't remember who came over. All I remember is grabbing my dad and my car keys and driving like a bat out of hell to the urgent care which was maybe seven minutes away. Because it was so early, the urgent care was closed. Quickly, I drove another 5 minutes until we reached the emergency room of the nearest hospital. Everything happened so quickly! The nursing staff took care of him at once and miraculously, they were able to stop the stroke in its tracks. Nobody but God! My dad fully recovered from his stroke. However, the following month on, Father's Day, I took my dad to the local Veteran's Hospital's emergency room. His arm had been paining him since the stroke. After numerous tests and scans, we were hit with yet another devasting blow. The doctor saw a mass on one of his lungs. Wait, what? I thought, there is no way God would allow this to happen. Nope! I'd lost my mother, my marriage, my grandmother and now I'd lose my father?? NO! I had a few choice words for God on the ride home from the hospital that night. My dad told me that he was "terrified." I encouraged him as he'd done me many times before, to believe that God was with us. Well, God was indeed with us but, my dad's test would still come back positive for Stage 3b lung cancer.

      There was no way for me to process all that was happening; it all manifested so fast. My dad was given chemotherapy and a couple of radiation treatments; which would prove to be a futile effort. On September 29, 2015, my parent's 43rd wedding anniversary, my dad, Fred Taylor, died. The man who truly understood me and had been in my corner my entire life. The dude who could tell a story and have everyone in the room crying with laughter. The man who survived the Vietnam War and overcame an addiction to alcohol. My only surviving parent was now…gone. So…much…pain. What was the purpose?? At the time, I could not process the pain I was experiencing. "How could God have allowed this to happen?", I thought. What could have possibly been the purpose for all this pain?

In the days, months and years that followed, I thought about dying every day. Every, single, day. Then, one day, I felt something I thought was gone forever; hope. After speaking with a close friend of mine who'd just experienced the sudden loss of a loved one, I realized the reason I was given such a heavy load to carry. I found myself in this situation often. Sharing my story with women who were ending a bad marriage, friends who'd loss their parents or grandparents. People who would ask how I could possibly smile after all I'd been through. My answer was always the same; but, God.

Despite losing three of the most important people in my life, my Mom, Dad and Grandmother, I've been blessed beyond measure! I purchased a new home, got a promotion at work, spend quality time with friends and family and have somehow found a reason to continue to smile. More than anything, I realize that all that pain provides genuine purpose to my life. Instead of stifling me, I use it to catapult me forward into success. I am no longer bound by crippling anxiety nor do I obsess about dying every minute of every day. I have come to understand that in life, there will be pain; however, the purpose of my pain, I believe, is to help others to heal. My life is a testament to God's promise that weeping may endure for a night, but joy comes in the morning. It's morning!

-Janise Taylor

CHAPTER FOUR

Fathered But Daddyless

Webster's' dictionary defines the word father as a man who has begotten a child. Coincidentally, the definition of "daddy" means the same. But for me, the word "daddy" takes on an entirely different meaning from the word "father". When I ponder on the word "father", I refer to it more as a biological term. Let me explain further why. When you look up off springs in anatomy and biology books, nowhere in there does it state that a child is created by a "mommy and a daddy". It refers to off springs being birthed as a result of a union of a man and woman, that become a "mother" and a "father" upon the birth of the offspring. In essence, I use this to support my theory that "fathers' and "daddies" are TOTALLY different. Now that we've gotten that out the way, allow me to elaborate further on how I knew that I had a" father" all of my life but not necessarily a "daddy".

I was born in the year of 1977 to Iris McRae and Wayne Bostick. This may sound crazy, but I knew, and I was born into a union of love at a very early age. Not sure if it was a union of love between my mother and father but I knew that more than anything else, my daddy loved and wanted me. Not only did he want me, his family wanted me too. I was my father's first child and my mother's second. I can imagine that my mother's thoughts were "What am I going to do?", when she found out that she was expecting her second child. She already had a 4-year old daughter that resided with her parents in North Carolina and here she was pregnant with another child over 500 miles away. I can imagine her even possibly wondering how in the world she was going to tell her parents and family that she was pregnant yet once again. Nevertheless, I am positive without a shadow of a doubt my dad was ecstatic. His thoughts may have originally been, "How am I going to take care of this child?" or "Am I really ready to become a father?" Those thoughts diminish though, the day that his baby girl entered his world on June 22, 1977. Especially since, his first child was born just one day after his mother's birthday, June 21st.

When it was time to name the baby girl, he was allowed the honor of naming her Irene. The name "Irene" combined the last part of his name Wayne(-ne) and the first part of my mom's name, Iris(-ir). At last, here I was! A brand-new baby girl for him to love. Fast forward 4 years later, my dad and I were inseparable. I can remember him taking me to McDonalds anytime I wanted. I can remember him taking me for car rides to see my Grandma,

Granddaddy, and the rest of his family. More than anything, I remember always being surrounded by love. Not only by him, but by his family as well. I simply remember being and feeling...HAPPY! So, on that life changing day back in 1982, my parents had the fight that ended all fights. My 4-year old self was definitely not prepared for this. I do not remember all the details of the fight, but I knew that something was terribly wrong. I remember my dad leaving out of our home and my mom rushing upstairs. Up and down, back and forth she went. It lasted for quite a while. Around this time, something in my young mind finally made me pay attention to what she was carrying. It was a trash bag! She was throwing clothes in a trash bag! At that moment, I had my first ever revelation. Something was terribly wrong, and my life was about to change. Never and I mean never would anything be the same.

    Isn't it something that you can repress innate objects that you've stored in your psyche for over 30 years? That's exactly what I've done with U-Haul trucks. Till this day I still feel an uneasiness when I see a U Haul truck or dealership. I remember my mother's brother, my uncle, coming to pick my mom and I up from our duplex in a U Haul truck. In and out they walked out of our house, carrying almost the entirety of the house out every time. I remember my dad and I standing aside looking at them do so. I so wish I could remember the words my dad was telling me at that time while we watched both of our livelihoods being packed up in that U-Haul truck. I like to imagine that he was trying to cram as many "I love you's" and "Daddy will always love you's" that he could in my mind for future storage. My dad pleaded for my Mom not to do this, but it had been decided. This part of my life was ending. We were no longer going to be residents of Virginia. We were about to climb up in that U-Haul truck with my uncle and set forth to North Carolina where I would be assimilated into my "new family." Those last moments shared with my dad are ones that have been instilled in my memory for decades. I remember how his hugs felt. How he smelled and how his mustache felt on my cheek when he kissed me for the last time. Then after climbing in that truck, just like that, my life with my daddy was over. My heart sunk. I missed my daddy almost immediately but more than that I had a strange feeling that that special bond that my dad and I shared was now over, to never be reignited again. In a flash, I had transcended from having a daddy, being a "daddy's girl" to just having a father. That day, a part of me died. That day I started my grieving process of losing my daddy. That was the day my daddy died.

When I moved to North Carolina, my first thoughts were, "This place is strange." When I first entered the house, my mother's relatives gathered around me. I was not as eager to accept these unfamiliar people and this unfamiliar place though. My mom tried her best to make my transition as smooth as she could, but I had this void in my heart that nothing could replace. That deep feeling of security and feeling safe was missing. In the infamous words of Dorothy from the Wizard of Oz, "Toto, I don't believe we're in Kansas anymore."

Going back "home"...for the FIRST time

When I arrived at my grandparents' house, my mother's

parents, it was nothing like what I had grown accustomed to. Where I use to be familiar with sidewalks and streets, I had to now familiarize myself with gravel, red clay dirt, and lots of grass. I had to be careful where I played outside because I was always being warned about "getting on a snake" versus back in Alexandria I had to only make sure an adult was watching me while I played in my front yard with my friend from next door. The new environment was very overwhelming to say the least. However, the one most significant and noticeable thing that was missing was MY family..my grandparents, my aunts, my uncles, my cousins but most of all my DADDY! My daddy was missing. I didn't have that one person whose arms I could run into when he or I came into a room. I didn't have that one man that I could run to when my mama said something that hurt my feelings. I didn't have that man that would swoop me up in his arms and play with me. I didn't have that man that would let me ride my tricycle through the house while he would be on the back of it pushing me along. I didn't have my daddy.

Transparency moment, I can remember my 4-year old self saying to myself, "My daddy is coming to get me. He's not just going to leave me here". I remember waiting, initially very patiently, and then increasingly becoming despaired. During this time, I started experiencing the "grief process" for the first time in my life.

The Process of Grief

Research indicates that there are levels of grief that we all go through. According to the website, PsychCentral, there are five stages that we will encounter. Those stages are as follows: Denial, Isolation, Anger, Bargaining, and Depression. The first of these stages or reaction is denial. As a little girl, I can recall playing outside by myself, due to being a loner. I constantly would look down the long winding driveway from my grandparents' house. Although I played a lot outside using my vivid imagination, I never missed a time to stare down that long driveway before I went into the house to see if a car with my daddy in it would show up. I was very adamant about my daddy one day coming to get me. No one could tell me otherwise. However, by the time I turned 10 I realized that he was never coming. The denial period was over for me. Isolation is supposedly the next stage, but with my experience I can say that isolation accompanied all of the stages of grief for me and still does. I was constantly isolated as a kid, voluntarily and involuntarily. That's just how it was. The times that I voluntarily isolated myself, I used as time to reflect on memories of spending time with my daddy. However, the older I became the more those memories became obsolete. I isolated myself and kept these feelings to myself because I felt like no one in my family could understand or better yet, even cared. Besides, those were precious memories that I chose not to share with anyone.

Anger is the third stage of grief and this one I did not experience until I became much older. I remember when graduating from high school, my former daddy, now father, attended my high school graduation. Since it had been quite a while since I had a daddy at this point, I was angry at this man, now known as my father, for trying to step back into the role of daddy. What made it even worse, he revealed to me that he now had other kids. WHAT??!! You mean to tell me that I not only lost my daddy, but I lost him to other kids? How could he? Wasn't anyone familiar with the golden rule, "The first and oldest child is the most special?" I was not only angry that I lost my daddy, but that I lost him to some other kids that were able to claim him as theirs. Ok, here's the second transparency moment. I still carry anger about that. I am still angry that my father didn't think I was fit to no longer be a "daddy" to, but he could go and be a daddy to other kids. Where is the fairness in all of that? The next stage of grief is bargaining. There were plenty of times that I did this. During my times of isolation, I remember asking God if He could just allow my daddy to come and get me or allow me to have my daddy once again. During my bargaining process, I promise I would for the rest of my life be a good girl. When I realized that this method was not working, I became discouraged once more. My reality was slowly but surely becoming very clear. There was nothing I could do or give to gain my daddy back. The last stage of grief but one that has had the most significant impact on me is depression. Thinking back over my childhood I realized that for the majority of it I was significantly depressed. I don't know if my mother realized this and felt helpless on what to do about it. Or if she was dealing with her own personal issues about having to uproot her life and move back to her small hometown. At any rate, I knew for sure that I was and I occasionally still am.

Losing A Daddy Then A Father

I lost my daddy when I was four years old and my father

when I was 30. This means that I grieved the loss of a dad twice. From the ages of 4 to 30, I experienced significant trauma in my life. Molestation at the hands of family members twice, bullied, emotionally abused and rejected by loved ones, and the list goes on. Each time I experienced a traumatizing event, I would always think to myself, "I wonder what my daddy would do if he knew about this or was here?" When I got my heart broken due to searching for validation in boys and men, I longed for the capability to be able to go to my daddy and say, "Daddy, he hurt my feelings, now go make it better or make it stop hurting." When I experienced times that I felt insecure or unstable, I longed for my daddy's touch that always made me feel safe, secured, and loved. I never got that. At the age of 28, my father attempted to become a daddy to me again. However, in my mind it was too late. I felt like the times where it was very prevalent that I needed a daddy had passed. There was nothing else for him to do. I no longer needed a dad, better yet a father. In my own words, "I was good". When I was 26 and got married, my father unexpectedly showed up to my wedding. I was livid! Not only did I feel like it was rude, I felt he had no right to be there. I purposely sent his sisters and brother invitations and not him. So, when he showed up and had the audacity to be upset that my mother's brother, my uncle, was walking me down the aisle, I sanctimoniously told my mother, "He had already given me away once, I didn't need him to give me away again." Yes, I said it out of anger but a part of me truly felt that way.

  Now that I am 41 years old, I can now admit that I miss having a daddy AND a father. Not having a daddy in the majority of my life has taken a toil on me. I have fears of abandonment, rejection, and not being accepted. Because of the fight that my parents had that caused the break up, I have problems and issues with proper ways of disagreeing or handling conflicts. Whenever I have disagreements, in my mind I believe that is the end of a friendship, relationship, or simple interaction with someone FOREVER! I think about how the absence of a daddy caused me to be very bitter towards my father. If I could turn back the hands of time, I would now accept his apology. I would try to understand that sometimes it's easier for some men to just be a father and not a daddy. I would later find out that my father was fighting his own demons and was not in a position to no longer be a daddy to me. I don't know if it was because he knew that he lost his little girl and that played a toil on him or what. Nonetheless, I know this to be my truth. I was blessed to have a daddy AND a father at least in one part of my life. Do I still grieve the loss of both? Absolutely, however I am learning to cope losing both and seeing the blessing in it all!

-Irene McRae

CHAPTER FIVE

Still Standing

We all have seasons in our life time and what we do in that season is up to you. The saying season, reason or lifetime comes to mind. I have heard this phrase for most of my adult life. The changes that we have endured because of the seasons of life and change has prompted me to look at transformations in my life; the circumstance of my grief, and how these changes affected the outlook and the future of my life.

I can remember my first instance of this phrase coming true was while I was college. You meet and befriend so many people from all different walks of life; color, creed, and religion. I made many relationships with my college peers, but some were more special than others. I joined my sorority, Zeta Phi Beta Sorority, Inc. when I was 19 years old; and what an accomplishment! I had formed connections with woman that would last a lifetime. In this, I was now on my way to learning how to make friends with others in my sorority and in Greek life. This was such an exciting time in my life that I was all in and found this season to be wonderful. As I was navigating sorority life, I began to become a young woman. In doing so, I had the ultimate responsibility to make sure my needs were met and to be responsible for my own well being being away from home. I missed home but knew that this journey was one that I had to take.

This journey led me to special friendships within my sorority. I can recall really getting to know myself and how my membership would afford me perks that I had not had. See, I am the oldest in my family, so I did not have a big brother or big sister biologically to look up to. It was just me. So, joining a sorority gave me many big sisters and big brothers. There was one special friendship that I formed, and I will never forget it. This big sister taught me many things that I just did not know. I was given a beautiful friendship that extended beyond college. Sadly, after we left school, we lost contact with each other and did not communicate. We eventually found our way back to each other, but life had changed over the years. We were not the same people understandably; college changes people and this had indeed happened to us. We were not as close as we used to be, and I often wanted the past friendship back. I sometimes grieve for the friendship that we had. I still wonder if life hadn't happened, where the friendship would be today?

This has led me to the next instance of how grief can

shape your life. I was a Daddy's girl growing up. I am the first born to my parents and thus I was special. See I was born premature and weighed only 1 lbs. and 14 oz. I can imagine how frightening this was for my parents, pondering if something would happen as I begin to live in this world. We all have found ourselves wondering about some aspect in our child or young adulthood, that we just couldn't change.

Mine was why did my father have to leave this earth when I was 16 years old? The friends that I had that had their fathers around, seem to be very happy and looked forward to spending time with them because there was always a treat in store. I really did not know how this loss would affect me until much later in life. I know sit back and wonder about the lessons that I would have been taught and how I would have figured out the right decisions. It is almost the 30-year anniversary of my father's death and yet; I grief and sometimes mourn him. How could this be possible you ask? I have found that in my experiences traveling through this grief journey, you never get over the loss of a loved one; but you will always have your memories!

It is a process of how you choose to see the world after the loss that makes the biggest impact on whether you stand or fall. Are you still standing or do give up and lie down? Will grief take ahold of you or will you lose the fight to continue to live? This realization came as I was writing my chapter for the Awake Anthology that I have been honored to be a part of. The stories in Awake feature woman who have decided to come alike in their business, personal lives and beyond! This is a true testament of how coming to the realization and waking up to my purpose that helps me continue to the memories even when I am feeling down and are grieving.

Sometimes in life you are given opportunities that you never imagined or even thought you would be provided. I was given a gift when I met my beloved and we started dating. He was kind, loving, a protector and a good provider. These were qualities that I was looking for and found them in him. We shared dreams and we decided that pursuing these dreams together made perfect sense. This led to many days and nights of talking about how we would achieve these goals and what we needed to do in order to make them happen. This was just the beginning and I was looking forward to beginning this journey.

Then life really hit me like a mac truck! My whole world was shattered when he passed away suddenly. I was horrified and could not believe the words that I heard. I felt I was in a bad dream and someone forgot to wake me up! This was by far one of the most terrible days in life. How would I continue to move forward with the goals and dreams that we talked about and how could this really be happening to me? I was devastated; and could not even begin to figure out how to climb myself out of this dark hole I found myself in. I had some really trying times in the beginning of my grief journey and some regrets. I was hurting and found myself depressed and suffering anxiety. These are things that no one talks about when dealing with grief.

Grief happens to everyone, but it is a silent and unspoken. People deal with grief differently. Some become recluse while others lash out at others to mask the pain they are feeling. I decided after I recognized that I was in a dark place to visit my doctor to discuss how I can begin to feel better. We talked about mediation, therapy and groups. As a clinician, I decided upon grief therapy to help me to a better place. Utilizing techniques that I was familiar with helped a lot. I was able to process my feelings in a safe environment and began to work on me and see better days.

These better days lead to journaling about my feelings and reading books related to grief. I sometimes had homework which helped me to think about the circumstances of my situation and to use it for good. In doing so, o my journaling became sentences, then chapters and eventually books which I shared my experiences and experiences of others as they sought to find a positive light in the grief journey.

From here I began to do radio interviews, and even visited the radio studio to talk about what I have experienced and what I was doing to help others. I have created digital products and even shared a bit of me and my story in two book anthologies, all in order to help others in their journey. I believe one of the proudest moments to date was starting an online support group for others who have experienced grief and loss. This group is named, The Healing Group Community, and from their more started to unfold. This led to a podcast and a group to discuss and talk about what I was now called to do! I am now a grief advocate that helps others in their grief journey! I am proud of this accomplishment even though there is still some pain. My goal was to not waste the pain and to use it for good. I now speak about grief while sharing nuggets of what grief is and how I can help manifest joy in our lives.

As a clinician, this led me to begin grief coaching to offer support to others. I am still standing only because of the word of God! My walk with the Lord has taught me that there will be good and bad times; mountains and mountain top experiences, but through it all, my purpose is certainly helping others to live life better, to celebrate the memories and to know that there is certainly gratitude in the life that we live. I am honored and humbled that God would see fit for me to share my journey with others and I hope that even one person is touched by what I do. This journey continues to give me purpose and know that because of my beloved I am honoring his life while helping others to celebrate theirs.

-Cherie Barnes

ABOUT THE AUTHORS

Cherie Barnes

Cherie Barnes is a best selling author, clinician, speaker, child of God and founder of The Healing Group Community, LLC. Cherie is the author of 12 Lessons of Healing Through Grief and Conversations with God: The Devotional. Cherie is passionate about helping others heal from grief, trauma and loss due to her own experiences. As an advocate of healing, Cherie helps others find meaning in life and support positive actions. Cherie has a masters degree in Counseling and is a Board Certified Counselor.

Valrie Kemp-Davis

Valrie Kemp-Davis is the author of multiple culturally conscious, multicultural and anti-bias books that celebrates children around the globe. She believes in the traditions of the Djeli (Storyteller) and loves to record history while telling her stories in a contemporary, clever, and relevant manner. This has led her to work towards perfecting her gift. She is the creator of the cultural platform, The One Love Project. She crafts stories to bridge the gap between others advocating cultural diversity, tolerance and inclusion amongst the Children and Chidults of the Diaspora. Her books teach self-love and respect for others.

Believing in the power of education, and self-knowledge, she has sought to cross the Middle Passage to join hearts and hands for a common purpose of reclamation of history, social justice, honor, love and unity. She skillfully uses the power and passion of art as a medium to carry these messages and as a form of bibliotherapy! Val, as she is affectionately called was born and reared in Tampa, Florida. She attended Warner University earning a Bachelor of Arts degree. She double-majored in Communications and English with a minor in Psychology. Her graduate studies were in Criminal Justice Administration where she attended the illustrious historically black college, Clark Atlanta University. Her law enforcement career spans thirty years respectively with the Georgia and Illinois Department of Corrections.

Valrie Kemp-Davis is a Life Member and Silver Star of Alpha Kappa Alpha Sorority, Inc. and has held several offices within her local chapter. She is the mother of two Jamerican daughters, and an aunt to several nieces and nephews. Her love of children has also led her to become a surrogate mother to several children. Many kids in the East Chicago community "chose her" and her home as a safe source of refuge. All who have lived in her home, and left are working towards attaining their goals in life. Her philosophical brand was developed under the Carradice Collection imprint where her slogan is Collectively We Carry This and Embracing Cultures, Enriching Lives.

She firmly believes as we carry each other, we Big up ourselves by bigging up others!
www.carradicecollection.com

Michelle McKinnie

Michelle McKinnie, a Licensed Clinical Professional Counselor and Director of Outpatient Behavioral Health. With more than 15 years in the mental health field, she has developed a unique approach to mental health that empowers individuals to live whole, healed, and healthy. Though Michelle's resume boasts of extensive skills, training, and experience, her passion is rooted in the ability to help others, more specifically women, recognize their ability to thrive beyond their pasts. Her "helping nature" is evident in her work with community agencies and assisting those in need.

Among Michelle's repertoire of expertise is speaking. As a frequent Child Development Cohort presenter at Harold Washington College, she educates others on various topics such as trauma, shame, mental health first aid, and child abuse. Her presentation skills have also afforded her the opportunity to speak on various topics related to Mental Health and Self Care for professionals for the National Association of Social Workers (NASW).

    Michelle has now begun her own personal journey of healing post her MS diagnosis in 2015. The event that shook her world. Visit her blog at www.derorwoman.net that promotes "Love of the Imperfect Woman." This is essentially her virtual online journal on how God is "doing a work in her life."

Irene McRae

Irene is a blogger, a writer, author, a 2018 ACHI magazine nominee, PRAYER WARRIOR, and an inspirational speaker. She has co-authored the Amazon best-selling book, "Broken But Not Shattered 2 and collaborated on 2 audio anthologies. She recently completed a suicide anthology, which is a devotional. When she's not writing, she enjoys being a single mom to her beautiful N.C. A&T Sophomore daughter, traveling and going to concerts, going to beaches, and binge-watching "The Wire".

Janis A. Taylor

Janis A. Taylor was born in Chicago, Illinois. She was educated in the private and Chicago Public School Systems where she attended Lane Technical High School. Janis attended Illinois State University in Normal, IL where she received a Bachelor of Sciences degree in Family and Consumer Sciences.

Janis has devoted her entire professional career to the Human Services industry, as she is currently a Staff Development Specialist for the State of Illinois Department of Human Services, where she trains state and federal policy related to human services programs to employees of the state.

Janis learned very early on in life that her gift was that of encouragement. No matter the circumstance, she has always found a way to encourage others, even amid her own pain. Knowing that God has a special calling on her life, Janis acknowledged in early adulthood that sharing her gifts would not only be pleasing to God and help others but would prove therapeutic for her own healing.

After suffering several devastating losses in her life, which would eventually lead to a nearly 7-year mental and physical health battle, Janis decided to channel her pain into power. With the help of God, her family, friends, and amazing therapist, Janis has been able to emerge from the depths of grief into a life filled with hope, happiness and purpose.

Janis further uses her gifts and talents in her passion as a freelance make-up artist. She is the owner and chief artist of Another Pretty Face, Inc. make-up application services where she helps her clients discover their inner beauty through skin care and make-up application.

Janis resides on the south side of Chicago where she enjoys spending quality time with her beautifully talented 12-year-old daughter, Xoie.

Janis has made it her life's mission to continue to share her story with others who may be drowning in the darkness of grief, with hopes that they too will one day find a way to turn pain into purpose.

Janis can be reached at **janistaylor1001@gmail.com** and anotherprettyfaceinc@yahoo.com

www.ingramcontent.com/pod-product-compliance
Lightning Source LLC
Chambersburg PA
CBHW031422160426
43196CB00008B/1019